Greenland

By the same author:

Hummadruz
Animaculture
The Tree Calendar
Book of Shadows

Greenland

HILARY LLEWELLYN-WILLIAMS

seren

seren is the book imprint of
Poetry Wales Press Ltd
Nolton Street, Bridgend, Wales
www.seren-books.com

ISBN 1-85411-352-6

A CIP record for this title is available from the British Library.

The publisher acknowledges the financial assistance
of the Welsh Books Council.

Printed by Gwasg Dinefwr, Llandybie.

Cover photograph: Sylvere Hieulle

CONTENTS

for my mother

The Visit

The room is still and quiet save for the muffled pulse of my clock. I am listening for inspiration, for a soft footfall. I have arranged my body among the sofa cushions in a comfortable posture, upright and receptive. I have taken off my shoes.

I am surrounded by windows at this end of the room. To my right a glass-panelled door reveals the terrace now smothered in grass and seeded dandelions, their blurry white heads nodding. A dark wind rattles around the building and seethes through the leaves like waves breaking. The apple blossom has opened a little more since yesterday; creamy clusters dabbled through the green. But the sky has lowered its blinds, ready for a downpour. Petals whirl like snow.

Suddenly there's a thump against the lowest doorpanel. It's the unmistakable resonance of flesh and bone. I think I catch a glimpse of a grey curved back. As if someone had hurled a cat or a rabbit at the pane. Then there's a flick of movement and a squirrel is standing paws up to the glass, looking in. Her face is oval as a nut, her eyes pinpoint a question. Her tail is held like a plumed umbrella; her belly sports pale fur like an apron. The small splayed fingers rat-a-tat – is she asking to come in, or simply attracting my attention?

I make a beginning movement towards the door and the creature vanishes, back into the wind that brought her. I peer into the undergrowth and up at the laden branches, but there's no sign of her. I settle back into the cushions and roll a cigarette. A sound in the trees like a gathering drumbeat. Rain begins to fall.

Ode to Rain

Rain you are everywhere
filling the air with glassy molecules
and the slow hiss of your outbreath as you glide

pulling the sky around you like a hood
and wiping the horizon
to a chalky smear.

You hit the ground running and scoot along
till you find a way in
going under to where you gather

for another ride through wood and leaf.
You are blood of the earth and river food
and ocean seed, mud maker

mountain shaper, carver of rock and cliff
stone polisher, road shaker
yet so thin-skinned you shatter at a touch

each water-bead breaking over the hills
and rooftops, cracking open
like soft eggs spilling dew.

Rain you climb in from the sea
laden with sea-sweat and the siphoning
of forests, falling in multitudes

jostling and whispering all night
a water-engine vibrating, a water flute
pitched to a low note, a gutter murmur.

So I wonder, what are your plans for us?
Will you trample us like grass and wheatstalks
and bend our heads down like the heads of roses

or soften us like fruit and cover us
with a bloom of rot? Will you wash us clear
of all dirt and colour, edges blurred together

with trees, towers, bridges, houses
one liquid grey dissolving
like paint left out in the weather?

Rain you have shut your dark doors
you have drawn your curtains around us
you have made our days fluid and porous

we see the world through your lens
shrunk to a dot at the end of a cloud funnel –
a dim flicker of light like a fish's tail.

Soon we shall have to learn to breathe water
and stand like trees drinking rain
catching it in our outstretched palms

or else grow fins like every other creature
and swim the drowned streets to the river
spreading over the land, and ending up somewhere

unrecognisable. If this is your purpose
too bad: we'll grumble as we've always done
but though you beat on our tiles till they're worn

to shell-transparency, we'll gaze through them
at any gap in the clouds and see there
the first footprint of the sun.

Making Landfall

One morning you wake to a difference
in the touch of the air:
somewhere a door is open

the smell of the world comes in
and flutters round you
as if stirred by wings,

as if borne your way on a shore wind
to the deck of your narrow ship
after months at sea –

an imprint of what waits below the horizon
beyond the grey expanse
cold heave of water

to reach you now, coffee and motor oil
fresh flowers and new-baked soil
warm rub of concrete

an onrush of green, an invasion
of leaves and spices:
a tang of sweat follows

and the world arrives and immediately begins
to reassemble its forms
out there on the edge of sight.

On such a morning you notice the birds,
the shapes their bodies make
in free flight.

Flock

There they go, slicing across my window
milliseconds before the rush of wings
whose echoes sweep the glass

banking as they pass
over rooftops, quartering the gardens,
the street grid, the back lanes.

Caught in the searchlight
of the sun against a sky of slate
now they are changed to steel,
to airfix models painted and glued together

flown synchronous and smooth
as if pulled sideways by an invisible hand –

the drill and hum of feathers all vibrating
in unison, the drumroll of their hearts.

Somewhere a pigeon keeper
waits on them

releases them each morning
to dart into the day with a clap of plumes,
rising over the terrace
wheeling above the park

like a handful of coins tossed
skyward by a lottery millionaire.

He is the backyard warden who holds the keys
to unlock the trick of flight,
who welcomes them to the home-made loft at night

who measures every grain,
scours their clotted lime

cradles each quilled body in his palms
to check the swell of its crop
and gazes into the circle of each eye

fingers each scaly leg with clip and ring,
names them, calls them his loves,
his nest of doves

and presses his ear to the coop
at midnight, drawn to the murmuring
within, the downy shuffle

in the odorous dark.

Out With My Broomstick

I'm out with my broomstick in the pearly light
  between dark and day
  between sleep and waking
    the streets like ancient rivers
      lie open to the sky

I glide on my scuffed pole with its tatty broom-end
      sparse and no good for sweeping but still it flies
    a hand's breadth over the pavement
      trailing its battered furze

the stick itself is long and extends behind me
  ready for the children to clamber on
    the children I've come to ferry through the air
      perched in my wake like ducklings

    and here's a clutch of them gathered by a gateway
      jostling like leaves

if a breeze sprang up they'd scatter across the road
  but they turn their faces towards me
  in simple trust and expectation of magic
    that it may fall like a cloak protecting them
      from winds both low and high

so they embark one by one
  making the pole dip like a divining rod
  but we clear the ground and just skim over the privet
  startling passers-by
      we are held in the air by a wisp
      a sliver of thought

and now I've delivered my charges my task is done
  I'm free to fly my own way
  I mount the broom light as a cloud
    the day has turned
      with a fresh breeze from the sea

from somewhere I've acquired a small sail
   striped candy red and white
    fixed to the mast like a flag and billowing
      like the skirts of a parachute
        I feel its sudden tug as it pulls me upward
          hauled along by the wind

higher than ever higher than a kite
   the world reels out below me
     I am soaring solo over the suburbs
     drawn by the salty current a glitter of hail

towards the city blinking in its mist
    coming clearer with each breath

Hawthorn

The river thick with rain
pushes against its banks

and glides like heavy silk
smoothing the boulders,

each shoreline packed with trees
outdoing one another in bursts of green
in white bloom froth and foam

over the rushing water
all jostling together.

There on the far side
rolled and drifted into a still pool

the body of a sheep, bright as hawthorn
caught in the leafy shallows

the olive runnels

fallen in surrender,
its head down
and smothered in the river

that passes with the sound of soft thunder,
the rising pulse of summer.

Steering by the Stars

Nobody steers by starlight any more:
we're too clever for that.

We've packed the stars away
in the dusty dark

turned the key in the lock.
Eyes down, we study our instruments

measuring our location
without benefit of heaven

the beasts above us, the ones
with fiery faces

blotted out by light.
We have banished night from the world

who needs it? It belongs
out there with the past

with the star names
of the Magi, who saw

the eyes of the Bull and said:
Aldebaran. Elnath.

Dubhe they said, and *Alioth*
and *Albaid*, the haunches of the Bear.

From the East, a long slow caravan
sets out across the desert

ships navigate the wastes
of the open ocean

and in the empyrean a blaze
of beings journeying

along with them, and Pegasus
is beating his four wings:

Scheat, Markab, Algenib, Alpheratz.
Heroes of old, the Archer

his bow stretched *Nunki* to *Kaus*
and the Hunter with the jewels

in his belt: *Alnilam,*
Rigel and *Betelgeuse* and *Bellatrix.*

In our age they glimmer wearily:
the Hunter with his dogs

Sirius and *Procyon* is redundant
eating burgers, watching Sky TV.

But the old names still resound
like incantations, syllables

of power. Just say it: *Acamar* –
a breath of incense on the night air.

Here are the citadels and palaces:
Alphecca, Al'Nair

Zuben'ubi, Tower of Justice.
Ankaa, the burning Phoenix.

And then the warriors:
Kochab, Polaris, Menkent, Rigilkent

conjured from their strongholds
in the hills, armed with their scimitars –

Schedar. Shaula. Enif.
The fixed stars. They flash crimson

gold and purple, sapphire, emerald.
They spin and twirl, coming to life, pulsating:

we're being watched, the pressure of their gaze
stinging our scalps like rain.

And now the summoning-spell
the words of sorcery:

Mirfak. Denebola.
That's when we all look up.

The Blessing

In this house at dawn
as the first plume of light
brushes the windows

something stirs
in the blind shadows
where sleep has roosted

all night, and moves around
corners, through doors: a creak
on the stairs, a murmur

of water in the plumbing
and a feathery sound
from the dust, a shuffle of quills.

After hours lying dry
and locked in wakefulness,
this hour between dark and day

with its pale glimmer dissolves
the threads that bind you
taut, so they melt at last

and drifting you hear the house wake
around you and preen itself
discreetly, a passing rustle

that shakes and settles
into its morning pattern:
a beady watchfulness

taking over, making it possible
to lie back and let sleep
carry you where it will

while a downy radiance
slowly fills, and unfurls
through the room as you slip past.

A Study in Grooming

She alights on my lap, while my attention is elsewhere. This is her predator's instinct: to make her move in the gaps between consciousness. And so she takes possession of the body of another creature. My legs for instance, now a grooming platform on which she balances lightly, poised to skitter off at any disturbance like a leaf in the wind. She turns her head to catch the smallest sound, whiskers perked like radar. Already there's a dreamy film over her eyes as they focus inward, her sight enclosed in herself as her ears watch the world.

Next she lifts a leg and begins to wash. She is still light and airy, resting the smallest area of her body against mine. She leans on one hip and wrist, inclines her neck in an arc, and slips out a rosy tongue. She works from the haunch down, long strokes over her leg extended like a ballerina's, down to the starred toes. Then she turns her face towards the sole of her foot, and runs her tongue over it, curling the toes inward.

As she does so she tastes the places she's walked this morning: the kitchen floor, the concrete path skimmed with rain, the greenish flavour of algae. She tastes grass and soil, absorbing their messages: spring coming, rain soon, whiff of tomcat musk, he's been snooping again, and she wipes it clean, deleting all information from the compact disc of her foot. A rewound tape, clear, ready for new imprints. I watch the tip of her tongue as it burrows into the frill of fur that borders each oval pad: muffled footsoles like a polar bear's. Then she chews on her claws with a sound like stripping bark.

Cats tongues look soft and dewy but their licking surface is covered with minute barbs that snag in their fur and trap grit and dirt and loose hairs and parasites, all of which they swallow, missing nothing, eliminating everything. Sometimes in her grooming-trance my cat licks my hand, and my flesh shrinks from the rasp yet welcomes the moist caress. Is this an accident, to mistake my skin for her fur? But afterwards she opens her eyes, raises her head and looks into my face, gauging my reaction – and my skin must taste of me, as hers does of her; she knows the difference, though she may wish to blur it, to mix our scents, to taste herself on me.

Abruptly she turns from her foot to her body, to rummage the thick black fur of her flank, rolling onto her side and committing more body surface onto mine. Her eyes are semi-closed, two gleaming slits in the dark shut face, and her head bobs rhythmically. She pauses, lifts her chin, and appears to listen. She listens for the signal to direct her to the next area, and darts her tongue towards it – the lower spine now – and she twists her torso with a gymnast's grace, doubling herself with no effort, braced on her front paws. This done, she listens again before relaxing, slowly shuffling down onto her stomach. And immediately she becomes heavier. My legs are pressed into the cushions beneath her weight.

Head down, she continues to groom, but the rhythm is slower. A few sweeps over her chest, and·last of all her front paw. Just one; the right one. I realise that her grooming has described a skewed ellipse: from back left leg, slantwise over her body to her chest and right forepaw. Later, after a short sleep, she'll roll on her back and nuzzle her abdomen, back legs splayed; this is when she's totally at ease and safe, exposing her soft underside. And so she completes the circle.

As she cleans her forepaw I see again how like a hand it is: four long fingers and a low thumb, each with its hooked tool. The pads are sensitive as palms, and when I touch them she curls her digits and grips my finger – not the blind grip of a baby, but with adult deliberation, a tender acknowledgement. But sometimes she'll push my finger aside in reproof or irritation. I learn when to touch and when not to touch.

For a time I am favoured as platform and nest, immobilized on the couch. But this is a morning nap, not her long evening sleep, and maybe she senses my own need to be up and doing. After a while she stirs, licks herself briefly, and I can tell by the sudden decrease in her weight that she's thinking about transferring herself elsewhere. And sure enough, she's up on her toes in a final stretch, and she's off.

A little later, I see her curled on a chair near a radiator. I speak to her as I pass, and she tilts her head slightly and opens one lemony eye and gives a faint, closed-mouth chirrup before subsiding again. I walk on into the kitchen and begin the ritual of making tea.

The Voices

This summer's gang of jackdaws has arrived
to roost in the opposite trees.
Dawn is rent with a hundred metallic squeals
and electronic yelps
and the scuttle of claws
on tiles, a hooligan
tatterdemalion clatter.

All day they squabble in the leaves
or patrol the air in uniform
black, in twos and threes
but sometimes in flocks
joyriding, screeching and turning
the sky dark and feathered.

Each year they come before the apples ripen
and stake out the garden
fighting over the fruit.
If you clap at them, they'll rise
in an indolent flap
crying their gleeful *Fuck!*
at will from the rooftops.

They are the looters, the stormtroopers
the vagabond leaderless army, the boys in black
unredeemed by the magpie's heraldry,
or by the low Tibetan chant of rooks
in their treetop monastery,
or the jay's fleeting blue,
or the raven's throaty laugh, his spread fingers.
They are mobsters, a demon crew
the spawn of Mordor. Which is all to say

I killed my first jackdaw the other day.

It was the voices in my head drove me
to murder: the yammering
going on and on.

. The cat had grounded one,
wounded its wing so it flopped and bounded
over the grass, a hunchback
wrapped in a feather cloak.
The gang swept screeching, each one a witch
in birdform, a slice of shadow
thirsty for blood. The cat was no good:
each time the wings lunged, he flinched
and hid in the rhubarb.

In the shed I found a length of pipe
heavy enough. My heart tightened
and shrank to a gourd,
a rattling pod. The bird edged
sideways, glimpsing its fate in the grip
of my hand on the rod, my swung arm,
spread its wings in alarm

but too late: the blow struck.
It lay on its back, its throat pulsing.
I tried to turn it over; it resisted,
coiling its spring. Inside
there were cogs and wires, transistors,
its circuitry convulsing

though I hit it again and again
its throat bobbed still.
So I crouched and whispered
just die! – and the bobbing stopped.

And the voices stopped. Over the trees
silence. Since that death
we sleep through the morning:

though the robot troops fly past
they won't land here, won't drop so much as a feather –
not while that straggler
hangs by its heels from the beanpole
flying straightwinged, bedraggled,
tethered to the rain and the stiff wind.

Menai

from a painting by Tracey Williams:
Stone wall, Castle, Flat roofed house, Palace, and Monument

The hills breathe in, and rise
then dive for the sea,
lifting their heads to the sky for the last time.

All winds are visible
from here, and the island
beckons beyond a cleansing rush of water.

We sit in branchy shade
this side of a wall
that writhes uphill, stones lapped like scales

or river coils
pulsed from the summit,
a torrent between two landscapes.

A seamless barrier:
yet that one has crossed over
into the warm light of the final field

where she stands white
as quartz, a statue
of herself, her back to us and the land

gazing into the void
of blue that shines and spills
over the edge of the frame, the brink of sight.

Beasts

i.m. Anne Szumigalski, 1922-1999

1

Midsummer wakes her, scooting up its blinds
in the small hours, letting the light in

and she wonders what kind of creature she's become
since she went to sleep in the heather clumps
guarded by feathery bracken

whose sharp and spicy smell tugs at a door
that opens just a crack to show a small girl
with scratched brown legs under a cotton dress
far on another hill

She blinks and yawns and stretches to test herself:
her body sprung like steel
yet supple as water, settles itself around her

and here are her four feet with their sheathed talons
the soft dark pugs beneath

She slips out her tongue to explore her nature
rasping the pale fur of her underside
the nipples like wrinkled buds
the closegrained yellow hide

Today she is a lion, she decides at last:
and she swishes her tail to prove it

2

Yesterday she was a spotted sow
nosing among the stones for roots and tubers
grunting in her joy

but now her desire is keener, it springs inside her
cloudy and red like the smell of fresh blood

it draws her to her haunches in the gorse
her gold eyes scanning the fields, the farms, the roadways
for something to stalk and follow

She tries out a growl   she feels it gather
swelling purple like a thunderhead
it bursts out as a roar

She stands in a rippled dome, a hall of echoes
wondering at her power

3

All day she grows more substantial:
by evening she is able to startle a farmer
who takes her at first for a donkey, or even a calf
until she turns her head

Back home, and over his fright
he'll have a tale to tell of the lion on the moor
there'll be a paragraph in *The Western Mail*
a silly season story

It makes no difference to her:
she has forgotten that she was once a woman
who used to take an interest in such things
who used to wander the hills
or maybe across the wide and windy prairie

Tomorrow she may change into a bee
hovering between thistle and dandelion
her mind flooded with colours
her voice just a blur of wings

Asking the Bees

Bees in the cranesbill
murmur round my ears
I lean back to listen

Their conversation
wavers and swells
in busy syllables

vibrating the air
tumbling from the fuchsia
from its wide red mouths

Tell me I whisper
into the honeyed clamour
What is the news this summer?

Will the sun bless us
will my wish be granted
where does this way lead?

But the bees' predictions
are all of the colours of flowers

their weight and sweetness
and the shortening days.

My Father Swimming

1

In the cold sea his body
slid like a warm knife,
softened the water's slab
coming up buttery
and sleek, with the green
tumbling and rolling off his skin.

His arms flung out to grasp
one handful then another
of solid swell, held all
in a broad embrace
face buried in the foam
blinded with salt. He loved
the pressure of its tongue,
a pearl flicker running over him

like light. And lifting
his head broke the air
into splinters that spun and shone:
sky and land one swinging bright
transparency. No sound
but the red drum of his heart –
all senses drowned
save touch: the sun's hand
smoothing his back and the surface
of the sea. He'd forgotten me

but I was there too, perched
in the rocks stacked like houses
or smoothskinned animals
flushed with heat, sparked with mica;
glad to be high and dry and watching him.

They called it *The Tank*:
this scoop in the cove
granite walled, where the sea funnelled
and boomed, then lingered
pushing at rafts of weed.
Beyond, the Atlantic roared
and fell on the land.
Down here the currents
spread their webbed fingers, tugged
their nets. He felt the cords
loosen, and kicked free.

2

My father's affair with the sea
almost broke my mother:
always dragging us to some shore or other
some windswept headland
our faces whipped with spray.
His eyes the same blue-grey, the same distance.

Twenty years before, in the war –
a ship of prisoners, torpedoed
blew apart, spilled its guts, oil,
dying men, their captors.
My father swam all day
all night. His life fell away
with the ship, left him clean
of past and future, just a swimming creature
lost in the vast glitter,
the ocean's mirror
hung in deep space, swaying.

The friend he tried to save
stopped moving, became dead
weight, and slipped down.
My father would not drown,
the sea loved him.
He lay back, and rocked
like flotsam, cradled in brine.
Swimming to live, floating
an imprint on his cells
that one day would be mine.

At dawn he reached an island.
Fishermen hauled him in
gently, and turned him over.
This was his great adventure.
He never spoke of the captivity
that ground him to a shell:
a five stone man, still walking,
still believing that the sea saved him
for coming home somehow.

3

He never taught us to swim.
We taught ourselves, after school
in the public pool
floundering around the shallow end.
The water seared my eyes
with chlorine stink, I disliked it,
the yammering din, the big kids
shoving, barrelling in.

The sea was wild. It swept
my feet from under me, it thundered
over my head, filling my mouth with iron
the taste of blood; it slammed
against me with the weight of the whole world.

But to reach down with my feet
into a void: that was fear
of a different order, feeling death
close over me. So I watched my father
swimming with held breath,
his body blurred
to a paperweight feather
in a sea solid as glass;
until he rose, expanding
toward the surface, smashed through it,
took flesh again, and laughed.

It was the land that killed him.
The long, dry years
grew dense inside him
to an end that was ordinary –
landlocked, and slow.
The tide inched back and left
nothing but a shell, a carapace.
That shrunken face
in the coffin was not him:

he was off somewhere, away
swimming perhaps, with long
and easy strokes, carried
out to a shoreless space
where I cannot follow.

The Whittling

Ynys Enlli/Bardsey

The island gods have turned inward,
fenced with water, bounded by the sea.

They duck their heads below the parapet
of wind and grow hard and nubbled

as heather roots, gorse twists, they shrink
into stone that pokes through bitten grass

clenched just below the surface.
They are marooned from their spawning grounds

in the icefields, bereft of rivers
that tumble through the lands,

cut off from the community of forests,
branches meeting each other in the dark.

They slip down to the shore to watch seals
nightly they envy their fluidity

and the zest of the invisible flocks
of shearwaters that pass with stuttering cries

inland, then out again through the gate of dawn.
Gods of the forest banished to driftwood scraps

have grown small and mean. He knew it,
the human visitor who took a knife

and chiselled this lump idly
released the god in the wood

with long thick head, a mind of dried tissue,
drilled eyes, a gouged grin

propped by a window: icon of isolation
made and abandoned for the next boat back

to wonder why it was called
forth, washed by changing light and voices

of passing strangers. Picked up, held
in the hand and made doll-like,

it whispers through its mouth-slit
be still, be still.

Persephone

"Make an effort to remember..." (Monique Wittig)

1

I have been in the woods.
I know what goes on there.

To enter I must cover myself with moss
muffle my shoes in fur
and practise breathing a different mix of air,

closing the gate behind me.
I am observed by lifeforms
with and without eyes:
blunt nudge of fungi in my direction,

insects with crowded lenses,.
the radar of trees. Each footstep
disturbs a city; each heartbeat
releases consciousness for their inspection.

From every wood I take away with me
in miniature a whole forest
impressed on the underside of my skin.
The mud, the twigs are itching

just so I don't forget
out here in the present daylight
what lives in the shade,

what will spring up whenever I sink a spade
in garden soil and strike roots.

2

You wouldn't think it possible to forget
the footsteps following
down the track from the chalk ridge heavy with summer

me with my schoolbag mitching
away with the birds

down the long tunnel of the trees,
and then what happened when the steps grew closer –

but I did, I forgot it all
buried it in the woods
under a heap of leafmould and bramble scrub.

I fell asleep under the hedgebank
burrowed in damp sand

and woke in a different land
treeless, anonymous,
changing my face in a mirror,
rubbing dirt from my knees

and in my mouth the remnants
of scarlet pulp and seeds.

3

The smell of the man the worst
terror worse than fox-stink
or caged beasts in the lion house

his own fear white in his eyes
and his hands shaking

worse than the gag of earth
and the fists that pummelled

Now I know the dread of the wild
creature who scents the hunter
on a small shift of wind

4

My first wood was the pinewood by our house
that heaved its bulk in a flurry of needles,

the tousled heads of trees, their stripped torsos
rising all around us as we climbed

from the frontier of the lawn up into silence
and resinous air. I and my little brother

alone collecting pinecones, scrambling
through the bracken, in the cobwebby light

the needle drifts, the cones with their open petals
dry as shells in our hands, the clumps of heather;

and once in midsummer dusk I saw from my window
a freckled deer with her fawn step over the threshold

into the shadows following our tracks
to the otherworld, until they disappeared.

5

Down in the undergrowth I became a bird:
I leapt up able to fly

scattering bits of stick and dead woodlice
and flakes of bark and leafdust.

Far below the sound of a voice shrieking
while I was perched on a twig
my face hidden in oakleaves

until my murderer blundered away uphill
and the trees swallowed him.

I sped on my new wings over stones and roots
to the hill foot, and I was light
and brilliant as a particle of sun

as I passed the great yew with her many children
electricity on the run

and over the railway I was a blur of feathers,
a tremor through the foxglove pinnacles
and the gate clanged after me and I was gone.

6

After descent, I hope for resurrection –
already
it's happening piecemeal

finger by finger
tooth by lip by hair.
In fact I am almost there:

daily I make myself
reassemble
flesh from the close-packed earth.

And this is labour,
building layer on layer
extricating myself from the tree-shadows.

Slowly, there are changes:
the pain in my neck has gone
that came from clenching myself against the blows.

One day my head will clear
and the last cuts will close.

7

I have been in the woods –
the dancing-floor of the beechwood, its maze of pillars,

wet tangle of a Welsh wood, never far
from the sound of water,

Boskenna Wood with its boulders
and the sea seething through,

the wood where I wandered lost
among darkening yew,

and the wood with a well in its heart,
the spice of ground-ivy
where something made paths.

Every wood I enter I cloak myself
in a dun pelt with pricked ears
and far-spaced eyes

stepping high and gently probing
between the trees,

my fine-tuned fibres crackling
and humming all over my body

picking up scraps of words,
a scrambled undertow of conversation
or maybe a flicker of music
coaxing me sideways off the beaten track,

never afraid but always curious
and watchful for what might come
out of the crumpled ground to claim me back.

A Lap of Apples

Looking for drowned apples
sunk in October seagrass
wet and salt with rot

I wonder what I'll find
in the rooty shade:

firm fruit just slit its skin
oozing white sugar-foam
bruised thumbprints still new,

drill-hole of a bird's bill,
all muddy but edible –

or pretenders laid
squat on a brown soft bloom
or a hollow woodlice home

or worse, those that lurk
under my shoes
blackened as leather balls

grenades in the dew.

A damp trawl nets some
sound ones, plus a few
hangers-on from the trees

to add to the store. Daily
the box fills, and the scent
of apple-ferment rises

cries *eat me* – peel, core,
make pies, make crumbles,

jelly rose glow, sweet
pulp to bag and freeze
and wine, wine....

But what if I don't have time
to deal with this glut?

I'm not the first to know
guilt over apples, regret
over all that's spoiled

all that tumbles into waste.
Did Eve and Adam lose
Eden the day they said

Such a pity this tree's unused!
Let's put this lot
to work for us – in their leafy aprons
bagging up windfalls?

Well if I know God she's no
housewife, she'd rather dance
than sit with a lap of apples

Slattern, she'll let the mess
take care of itself; which of course
it does – the leaves, the fruit

the lives all fallen
into rich mulch.

Making Man

Something of stone, the heft of it
in your palm, the way it moulds
to the curve around your thumb –
the Venus mount – yet resists it:

something of wood, the rasp
of bark on your arm, the damp moss
smell, webs of xylem
packed sinewy in your grasp:

something of earth, the dense
and crumbled soil, dirt in the whorls
of your skin, muddy boots in the hall,
that clod indifference

out of which things grow
haphazardly, and jostle into form:
and something brutish too, the tossed horns,
rank sweat, stamped hoof, a bellow

in the frost, the way they stand
to piss, the hairy pelt and jaw,
and the old thrust and tumble;
the way they squint at the wind.

Inside, we're all the same:
thinking, and passionate,
bloody and soft, and fearful;
we all lie down to sleep, we all dream.

But outside it's the other, stark and raw
that makes the sap rise; the them
and us, the border, brother earth
and mother sea colliding on a shore

salt-tongued and dangerous.
So we said *let us make man
from our own flesh* and let him be
stone, wood, and beast for us.

Fintan

O fish those silvery inestimable creatures
slices of light in all colours
bent by the lens of the sea

So old and wise their minds
supple as water

Those unblinking eyes
have seen everything invisible to us
the aeons flickering over their membranes

Their gills open and close
like mouths speaking
behind a glassy screen

Deafened by air and our brains' static
we must interpret their words
by the sweep of their tails   the gestures of their fins

The Salmon in his pool under the trees
sunflecked and still
is spotted with signs   if only we could read them

They are the bodies of our ancestors
their backbones are plumes of fern   we split them open
for their cool flakes of flesh

They part like the leaves of a book

*

We all come from fish
inside us the sea surges
we skim like clouds in an inverted heaven

We swim through the night ocean
shoals of us dip and curve in unison
thoughts ripple through our transparent skins
bouncing like echoes

These are our dreams in the frondy forests
frail bones of the dead settling into the sand

Picked clean by the nibbling lips of fish

Inside

for the Dark Age woman found in the dunes, Co. Donegal

However I appeared
after all these years
it's my inside that's endured

my inner self revealed
as armour, hard
and light and unpeeled

with my life rubbed off
in the sand, the soft
stuff melted, spindrift

web of nerves thrown
to the seawind, gone.
I am pared down to bone.

All my links are unfastened
like a necklace lost
in the dunes and darkened

to potsherd, woodcore.
Good craftwork, the jaw's
carved rack, the scapular

the bentwood tibia,
each ivory finger.
Here's the cracked spar

of my breast, the ribstaves
worked loose, and the cradle
that rocked my babes

is like a blown flower.
The skull is a door
that leads nowhere any more.

But my spine is winged:
now it's a kitestring
uncoiled, a garland

a skein of moths, a flight
of stairs, a rope, an exit
through the labyrinth of night.

The Badge

Finding myself after nights of grief and dread
in a room full of rainy light
knife in my hand, no-one can do this for me,
I prepare for the ceremony

I am about the join the community
of those who have removed and replaced their heads.

Cutting it off is easy, I feel no pain,
what's difficult is finding the thing again
wherever on the carpet it's rolled to.

Headless, but I see with shadow-sight
a fluid shudder of colours, images
which will soon falter and disintegrate
unless I reattach my head quickly

and I must do it quickly, it's not too late
while nerves and flesh are still living.

I'm trembling cold and bright
as a knife-edge, I feel high
and light as you do when shrugging off a pack
you've slogged under for miles. And there

on the floor it lies, I recognise the hair
tumbled and black, the face
turned mercifully aside, a glimpse of cheek and brow

that's mine all right so I take it
lift it like a warm and weighty stone
up to my neck and steady it in place.

I must wait now while vein and bone
and fibres knit together
motionless in case it all untethers
as round me the others gather

praising, giving me space. Thin fluid
oozes from the join – is this normal? They nod
yes, yes, don't worry, it's healing.

My lover wants to hug me, and I say no
not yet, this is still too new

but he leads me to a seat beneath the window
plump with purple cushions, he kisses me
and promises he won't disturb my head

which balances on its stem
like a flower just opened.

As he enters me I touch my neck
very softly and think of the scar I'll have,
the badge of those who've lost their heads
                              and regained them

a fine red necklace, indelible thread.

Worm Casts

for Gareth

On the lawn we practised wickedness
in whispers
searching

gently parting the blades
gummy with dew to finger
the scalp of earth

and finding brown whorls
curled like umbilicae
twisted in fleshy knots.

We'd handle them with precision
bringing each one closer for inspection
their body odour faintly rude
and warm in a child's palm

heads bent in conspiracy
laughing at our discovery
of the earth's orifice
its round deeds

our knees stained green from the sappy stems
secret and delightful as picking scabs.

Beneath us tunnelling worms
their blind snouts probing the grains
in darkness
feeding.

From a Stone

From a stone in my palm
I have made a bear cub

blind and hairless:
yet her pulse flicks warm
in the nest of my hand

and her long paws scrabble
against my skin
as she noses warm
and nuzzles in.

Soon she loses the shape of the stone
becoming flesh
and fur, with a voice of her own

so I can hide her no longer –
not even in the folds of my coat.

She plays like a kitten
rolls over, displays
the petal soft underside of her feet
and bares her teeth a little

yet her small bright eyes
are unreadable
as pebbles
or stars.

*

When the wind roars
from the forest
my bear lifts her head.

One day she won't come to my call
but with a curving claw
she'll trace a crack in the wall

and away she'll roll
into the leafy shadows

growing like a mountain
shaking heavy flanks
she'll become a presence:

the snap of a twig behind me,
the breath that follows.

Reynardine

"And if by chance you look for me, by chance you'll not me find:
For I'll be in my green castle – enquire for Reynardine"   (Trad.)

There was a time it dangled with her clothes
denned in the soft folds
between silk and wool, a touch of animal;

when it was the sly face in the wardrobe
peering from the slot
of a half-open door to whisper to me

from its dry mouth with the black ribbon lips
clamped on tooth slivers,
slant-toed feet stepping through thickets of coats

scuff, scrabble of claws on the bedroom floor
the red shape coming,
a nip of teeth on my neck before I woke.

There was a time my mother wore the fox
over her shoulder
her relic, dated as stays, from a lost age,

with glassy eyes and ears like shrivelled pods
flat to the wedge head
that grinned and nodded at me behind her back.

The figure wavers, dim and towering:
a whiff of camphor,
Nuits de Paris, and cats; the neat paws dancing;

an empty skin, boneless banner of fur
bodiless but wise
keeping an eye on me from the shadow side.

Gently now with the poor tattered bundle:
that sleek seducer
from the pungent woods reduced at last to this.

Fur

We were not made to withstand
this world, this cold.

Naked, we shiver
and still try to raise our lost hairs.

Without a covering
of sun or water
frail as the membrane of a moth's wing

we're bruised by the wind:

with an abrasion of frost the rot sets in
softening our sinews.

On days like these –
steel-bright, with showers of nails, gusts
buffeting like trucks on a highway –

I would not venture out
without these wrappings:

layers of fox, layers of cat, of snow
leopard gently dappled

around my shoulders, tail stroking the ground
with every step
a soft footfall

my face enclosed
in a cave of warmth, my hands

blunted and sheathed like paws.

I would not go
stripped bare to the horizon
in human form, erect and teetering,

but hunkered, keeping my centre
low and my scent blown over:

my thoughts shut down
to a narrow gleam
around corners, crouched in doorways,

brushing past you on the stairs.

Snow Story

for Anne Cluysenaar

Snowfall has rounded the hills
drawing them nearer,
plumping them like mounds in a picture book,
like the bowed heads of beasts

grazing in spindle thickets
wreathed in cloudy breath.

So she pulls on her boots and takes her coat
and goes out to the cold,
shutting her door on grief with no backward look,

her steps creaking gently on the snow,
the distant muffled rumble of a plane –
these are the only sounds

until she reaches the border of the wood
that crackles with silence and the soft
thud of snow from its branches,
a rustle from its heart.

But the hind is started:
a sideways glimmer
against the crossed shadow of birch and pine
white as heraldry,

white as the white hart in a tapestry
or the innsigns only without its chain
and its golden crown,

glancing with the eyes of someone known
from the other side of death.

Then with a pale flicker the creature's gone,
extinguished to a blank on the retina
leaving the woman frowning in the sun.

Nervously she stumps among the brambles
scanning the ground for symbols

and edged in ice she finds
two double slots pressed deep
where the hind leapt the hedge.

Now she can turn her back
on the wood, and trudge homeward
along the printed track

glad for the evidence of a beast's weight
carried on slender feet.

Walking to Greenland

We are walking North, strung out in procession. Like a village ramble or a small demonstration we spill along the road, straggle and huddle, stroll or stride, leisurely yet purposeful, moving on. Moving toward the cold, toward a darkness that blurs the horizon, closer with each step.

I am near the front of the group as we enter a township. There's a broad main street lined with clapboard buildings, shops with heavy awnings, and an old fashioned wooden sidewalk. The wind blows thin. It all looks shabby and tired. There are no vehicles, no people visible. Perhaps they're watching from behind the grimy windows, as we pass by. I turn to you and ask where are the children, they should be with us. You say they're with their friends, just a little way behind – they'll catch us up. Anxiously I turn to look into the following crowd, and see my son talking to a friend. I wave at him; he sees me and waves in reply. His sister is further back with some other girls. They're fine, they're fine. No need to worry yet.

As we leave the town there's a movement off to the left, from a waste lot strewn with abandoned cars and trash bins. It's a polar bear, coat faded yellowish in this halflight, plodding toward us. It heads straight for me, and falls in step at my heels like a dog. I am afraid. I know these bears. I know they often attack from behind, flinging their powerful arms round their victims' shoulders, grasping the head in their jaws, crunching down. I can feel the warm huff of its breath on my neck. I can smell the oily fish-reek of its hide. I can hear the steady pace of its feet on the road. But no-one else appears to notice the bear.

So I say nothing, and after a while to my relief the animal drops back and then it's not there any more. We walk on. It gets darker and colder. Where are we heading? The Vikings had a legend: beyond the extremes of ice, beyond the endless dark of winter and the midnight sun, lies another region, an earthly paradise. *Hyperboreas*, at the back of the north wind. Balmy, fertile, the hidden land, the promised place. *Greenland*. Is this where we're going?

But wait – we have come as far as we can go. Ahead of us is a barrier, a curving iron railing beyond which is a void, plunging to a black and seething ocean. Its surface is glossy as pitch; it moves up and down as if breathing. Gradually and one by one everybody lines up by the railing to stare at the sea. We fall quiet, stunned by its heaving darkness, the tight curls of foam that gnaw at its surface. White knots that appear and disappear. Someone comments that it's possible to cross this stretch of ocean, there are boats, but I shudder at the thought. The sea is swelling now, its movement strengthening.

Till I see it coming, a massive wave, blotting out the sky, towering and black, pressing forward, gathering the ocean into itself, unstoppable. I yell at the others to run, but some people are laughing in disbelief that any wave could be so vast. Others run with me, and I know that in a minute it will sweep over us, and what will become of us then? What about my children? I am distraught. Where are they in this mêlée? And now the wave is upon us, breaking with a roar that drowns all my senses.

I am tumbled over and over, but strangely the water isn't as cold or as wet as I expected. It's more of a mighty force that knocks me helpless, and then passes. All breath is sucked from my lungs; then I can breathe again, a rush of air that tells me I'm alive. I stagger to my feet, and see both my children scrambling up, unharmed, like everyone else. The wave has gone. The air and the sky seem lighter. Everyone seems exhilarated and refreshed: laughing, shouting, chattering. You too, safe as I am. Shaking salt water from hair and eyes, from clothes and baggage. So that was it, we say. We made it. So far, so good: so far, and all this way. A few dry flakes of snow powder the ground. And as for the sea, that has sunk down again beneath the barrier, swaying in its harness of tides.

Acknowledgements

Some of these poems have appeared in the following publications: *Poetry Wales; Scintilla; Poetry Ireland; Poetry London; The London Magazine; Metaexhibition.*